Outspoken Thoughts
Final Cut
Stephon Staley Jr

VP of Learning Resources: Life Experiences
Managing Editor: Stephon Staley
Academic Operations: Stephon Staley
Quality Assurance editor: Stephon Staley
Cover Design. Lulu Enterprises, Inc.

Published by Lulu Enterprises, Inc.
3131 RDU Center Drive
Suite 210
Morrisville, NC 27560

ISBN: 978-0-557-05277-6

www.lulu.com

Preface

Do not get the wrong idea. These are NOT poems; these are as the title says, "Outspoken Thoughts". Several of these thoughts are from development stages in my life therefore. Some of these thoughts you will need to consider carefully; take time to look into them. Always remember that most thoughts have a deeper meaning than what is on the surface. So read deeply, read well, and enjoy.

[§]

ISBN: 978-0-557-052

Table Of Contents

About the Author

Stephon "Deuce" Staley was born and raised in downtown Cincinnati, Ohio; on the corner of Race and Findlay Street with background roots from Aldridge, Alabama. Many people say that the people that come from this area are uneducated and ill bred. Due to the fact of high transgressions in the area and those living conditions in which people are raised upon. But as you read his thoughts and experience, you will see people from this area in a different perception. The thoughts here are unique and universal; and are meant to open up the rational part of the brain, which includes deep thought. **[§]**

Life
May '05

Slowly rising but dying, while dying and rising.
At no time will you be at the top.
But still you will slowly be dying.
Anticipating your next move on how to get money.
Robbing a man, selling dope
it's all hard-earned money.
No justifications for the wrongs that
we do. Judged by people that do wrongs
But not like, we do.
"He, who is without sin, cast the first stone".
But, when we stop to think, no stones should be thrown.
So how do "we" "the people" justify each other's acts?
Wait for the court system and leave it at that.
Intrigued by science and the study of religion,
We all live our lives in inconclusive decisions.
A constant fight over who's really right.
Putting all the facts together, both sides are right and
still we fight over unsolved decisions.
Realizing that life is an unsolved decision.
[§]

Pain

Jan. 06

Pain is real, pain is illusion, and pain is
what we all hate, the pain you touch,
the pain you see, the pain that makes
you ache.
The pain that makes you start to
cringe. The pains that make you shake.
The pain from the streets, the pain from
all the hate.
We start to live with all the pain, we start
to live with all the hate, and as days and
weeks go by it's ourselves we start to hate.
From all the tears and all the pain we really
start to think. That was daddy's little girl
and he raped her by the sink.
Should he die? Should he suffer? We
all start to think.
That pain is real, pain is illusion, and pain is
what we all hate, the pain you touch,
the pain you see, the pain that makes
you ache.
Holding life in your hands is Gods gift
to you and if you take that life away. ...
may God take yours from you.

[§]

Unknown Reason

Aug '06

The words that we express to each other are often; expressed in unspoken thoughts, body movement, written words,

and the look of; our treacherous eyes.

Wanting to tell them but, we are lost in fear, chased by those words that tell us they wont hold us dear.

Too afraid to open our hearts an express true emotions,

We treat others as nothing and cause others deep incisions within their emotions.

It is because of our encounters in life that cause us futuristic pain.

Too never really, love for as we feel, we have nothing to gain.

So we start to smile not out of laughter but self pity, because the one that would make us smile we neglect because of this pity.

Then time passes and how sadden we are, because of the one we just lost, to another; we are so deeply scarred.

To never really know if we would have been ever happy, sadden, abused, or even mistreated.

A teardrop falls for this unknown reason. [§]

Climax
Feb '07

Slowly starting to rise as her body rubs against mines.
Eyes locking, body tense. This moment shouldn't really exist.
Body glistening, room hot, and bed soaking wet,
mentally wanting more and more aroused is what you get.
Slowly we both start. In and out as we go,
flesh from my back in your hand; as you scream
"Give me a pillow".
Harder faster, softer, slower.
looking as you climax. Over your body I hover.
with no sheets or no covers. Falling to my knees pleasing
with intense pleasure. Switching positions is
where I give us both even leverage. One hour, two hour were
will we stop? Late night creep, afternoon lunch, and early
morning beating.
The sex that we have seems just like
mistreatment. Throwing, grabbing, punching and
still sensual loving,
moaning we both are in a sly like sensation.
The farther I go the more we feel temptation;
to take control of the other and; please their temptations.
Coming together once more, we both release our fire.
Now sticky and hot, and bed more wet, we roll over now.
Holding each other . . . . thinking of our next event. [§]

Accused
Feb '06

We gone take this back to
"Shoot! Don't! Please!" You no longer
hear the screams and the blood goes
Off the sleeve.
Children die because the elderly no
longer believe, in the society that put the
blood on the sleeve, loaded the gun,
pulled the trigger, and made
a man want to be a nigger.
Is this truly a society, where the unknown
source no longer runs the earth?
Who is God to you?
If I loaded a gun with bullets, and let
a blind man pull the trigger, how can
you figure I'm the killer?
Suicidal thoughts
caress his mind, and at times, he doesn't
know if he really wants to be alive.
And all he did was ask for a wish, a
death wish. Then he took his own life
with the wish.
And now you hold me here as the accused.
What do you really have to prove? That I am
As ruthless as the rest? John Wayne Gacy and
made up murderers like Hannibal.
How do we truly know I am not the killer? Because
we all know he was the one that pulled the
trigger. Think about it.
[§]

Continuous life

March '04

We are lost in emotionless thoughts. Take and hide our anger then think back before we even had thoughts.

Do we really know pain; only influenced through life's struggling times that sometimes seem like games?

People often envision the children that lived through birth,

hoping that if they die that will bring there loved ones back.

Then we think back, in the back of our mind,

"should I have died so another's loved one could have survived"?

This godlike fate often presses your mind, making you wonder when your time will arrive.

Slowly dying and living one day at a time.
Just trying to make it through these so called "interesting times".
We close our eyes and dream of a hope.
That maybe our life will get easier as days goes by.
We do our best and try to succeed, but in this crab like life only the strong-armed succeed. [§]

Feelings

Feb '06

So close! So far, but at the same time still close,
a destiny it is, but about it, we never boast.
Always around…a step or a pull away,
it has its own tendency to
make us act or feel a certain way.
Tears shed for the ones we have lost.
Always in our hearts. And in our minds,
They are often thought of...
People often cry, laugh, and frown
hiding their true feelings that will
Always be around.
Now sit back and think about how you
truly feel, because emotions are
a quest and you may lose in the end.
Creeping through the shadows and
grabbing for life. Some feelings that
you feel will have you losing your life.
[§]

A Women's Beauty

Jan '07

A women's beauty is, defined as such of that of an artifact,

A work of art. Something that is, sometimes lost and sometimes never found.

Many men often mistreat and misuse this beauty,

for the purpose of their own, that makes them seem like a motherless child.

This beauty I speak of is not an outer beauty

but an inner beauty that is; hidden from the outside world,

because of many problems that she has faced.

mainly from many man in her life of a bad distaste.

Man slowly breakdown the essence of a female until she slowly, but surely, truly in love with him and believes that he; her love is "the one".

She is so blinded by his" game" that she truly believes that

he loves her, in return for the priceless love that she has giving him.

On the inside knowing that he is doing her wrong but because of that great feeling of love in her heart he can never do wrong.

Until her soul is tired of, constant mistreatment and her body can take no more

all friends, family, and any other will be wrong for making comments about her loving and caring one.

In love, there are only those in love and all others will be wrong. [§]

A letter
Dec '04

Every mans fatal mistake is a look not a touch,
Which leads to lust, a whole of touching a whole
lot of fucking.

Yeah I got to close and got my heart broke, my
feelings hurt. I tried to tell you how I felt, and friends
is what you wanted to be? I took it in and told you I
was cool wit just being friends, but truth be told I really
wanted to just be your man.

A diamond in the dust I queen that I saw at work, I got
to close to you and you told me how to be with you I
had to work, I had to work my ass of just to be your friend
truth be told, I knew we be friends in the end.

Aren't many girls that I've met that's just like you funny, smart
intelligent and unusually, beautiful. So in the end if I hurt you I
really am sorry. But think about it how many guys out there
would say I'm sorry and mean that shit from the bottom
of they whole fucking heart? How could you tell me that you
want us to part.

I thought that me and you were one of a kind, you told me if we
had problems we'd work them all the way out to the shine,
How could you care, for me then send me a letter.
Telling me you met your ex in some of that Cincinnati weather,
Sucking, rubbing, teasing and touching but at the end of the letter
none of that shit meant nothing to you.

But I was your man, but I guess when I left you found another man
to walk and hold your hand. [§]

Dreaming
Nov '05

Is this really me or is it a
dream, where there is no death
and no dope fiends? People actually
getting along, doing things
right and living in homes. And not living
alone.
I open my eyes wider to see a
place where children are on the grind and
TV raises the children. And black people,
still believe in "the man". And people out
"doing what they can" but not doing
what they actually can.
Poverty everywhere, hidden by
society. Certain people can't progress
because those suicidal thoughts are grabbing at
them. As proper English is on a decline
single mothers and fathers are out there
crying.
Then I start to close my eyes
blue skies, no clouds, bright
sunny days children on the
pavement playing jump rope today.
No murders or crimes just smiles
And hi's.
Then I open my eyes, continually
dreaming of a place nonexistent to
my eyes. Do you see the crime?
[§]

Exploration
Sept. 07

Heaves and sighs of increased pleasure and pain.
She tears into his back trying to balances his game.
Hard but not faster, he maintains his speed
bringing each other to a new form of ecstasy.
The tension they hold is released through the thrusting,
kissing, pushing, and sexual location.
A reverse cowgirl, a Sicilian corkscrew
a pleasure for both sexes.
Led by images of what they shouldn't do.
The grabbing, the squeezing, the scratching and bleeding,
The crying, the screams, the biting, the sheets.
The climax they want, has yet been discovered,
a leg numbing, body trembling, eyes rolling, breath taking,
baby making, creation of unimaginable passion.
Hands moving attentively exploring every sensual spot.
The touching, rubbing, and feelings intertwined.
Bring us to an exploration exquisitely divine. [§]

Are You Black?
Feb '04

If you live in the ghetto and are low on money,
Are you black?
If the color of your skin is brown but your hands
and feet are white,
Are you black?
If your soul screams out hatred for the pain that
your ancestors went through, but today you work
for the descendants of the perpetrators of pain,
Are you black?
Until a person realizes that they are black because
Of the color of their skin and not the way they act
that person is ignorant.
Brains and individuality are the promoters of life,
blacks are not the only ones who have suffered hard times
and if you do not realize it is the way, you announce
yourself as an individual and not how you act or
The color of your skin. . .
You, yourself are… a nigger.
[§]

Who Am I?
July '04

I am quiet but loud,
I am peaceful but violent,
I can cover small spaces,
and I can cover large spaces.

To some I am beautiful,
To some I am atrocious.
I can easily kill or
can hold life in my great powerful
hands.

I have heard the holy prayers of many
and I have heard many prayers, unholy

I have been here longer than you and many animals.
I am not God.
Who am I?
[§]

Two Souls
Feb. 06

Two souls clashing , on the run, fighting for their lives
from an evil that threatens
their lives and it's pressing down hard. Crushing
these souls. Nowhere for these souls to go.
They're constantly on the move; so how can they eat?
The evil's getting close, so these souls duck into the shadows.
Thinking of a place where they need no
shadows.
Tears on their faces, feeling like giving up. Looking up
to the sky, only one thing gives them hope.
No one knows how they know about freedom.
All the souls know is that they're tired of this evil.
Freedom almost near. It's so damn close! When the
evil grabs them tight and won't let go.
A punch here, a jab there, fighting for their lives.
While the fear in their heart is stabbing them,
like a knife.
Freeing themselves from evil's grasp,
the souls take off in a furious blast!
Running hard and fast, they make it closer to
the light.
And the closer they get, the more
they can't fight. Because the closer they get, the
more they see that the evil they're running
from is their own family.
[§]

That Feeling
June '04

Sometime anger is pain.
Sometime pain is love.
But whatever the pain…
it hurts.
You can smile and act like it's not there,
or you can show it around
people that really don't care.
Whatever the pain is, it was introduced
by you, and in the end, it can only be
eliminated by you.
So close your eyes and really start to
think . . . should I continue letting this pain
continue hurting me?
Deep inside, tearing me apart.
When all you have to do is tear the pain apart.
And then and only then will this pain depart.
Open your eyes!
Where did this pain start?
[§]

Things Happen
May '06

Enchanted by the surrounding world we're in
constantly looking for that boy or girl,
and when we feel like he or she is right,
we put them in a box and give them our life.
Not only our heart, which they have for show.
But our life in general, which is just like a road.
Not smooth and short, but long and rough.
A continuous journey for those in love.
Times passes, enchantment wears thin.
The one you thought you loved now considers
you a friend.
Heart broken, lost, and carrying the world,
on your shoulders, your life seems meaningless,
and in your road a boulder.
Time will pass, and you will see in the end.
Your true love is out there and might be a friend.
So open your eyes and heart to see that you're last
Relationship really was not meant to be.
[§]

Together
August 07

Slowly he caresses her, spreading her slowly kissing her.
Intimate kisses to her lips, as he lovingly slowly lifts her.
Further, his tongue reaches, as she grapples him and straddles him.
As he cups her; and drinks her, tasting all of her passion.
Faster and slower, softer and lower, her body starts to roar.
She grabs him and screams "love I can take no more" in the middle
of her scream her as body goes numb, heavy are her lungs, and still
deep in her slithering, is his constant moving tongue.
Pain, love, and passion mixed into one.
A girl becoming a woman this story has just begun.
Her body continues to twitch, as he gently swallows her clit.
And explosion of candy, a sweet and sour unknown mix.
Licking and sucking, rubbing and sensual touching,
intimate thoughts of no protection, as they lose each other in a sought out destiny,
slowly he enters her, driving her on course
in and out, he thrust; who loves who the most.
Flesh in her hand as he lets out his roar
"love can I continue because I still have more"
empty and swollen intimately she purrs "five more minutes
and I be ready for your love" [§]

Explain
July 07

Tender kisses across her cheek, from her stomach to her thighs
to her lips, make her see, and eternity of love and expression of thought, to show
her you are different then most men that walk.
Show her the love that she sees in your eyes that you can sleep with her without
sex on your mind.
That you can hold her tight on dark cold nights, And hold her hand and just be by
her side.
Maybe she wants to be a beautiful queen instead of sexy like those women that you
see on the streets. To never be lied to, or sidelined by a friend.
A man whose not a boy who won't leave her in the end.
She wants that "one" that is not there for fun, but for a lifetime experience until the
story is done.
To make her smile for no general reason, or to give her flowers just at the change
of the season.
To laugh at her jokes, even when there not funny, but for self-satisfaction to know
that you care.
Explain my brothers why must this be, that most women in our world do not feel
complete?
As you answer this, please don't say
that woman don't want this ...
for this may be the reason you are lonely today. [§]

Her
April 06

A look is a stare that creeps into the soul,
in tales, as the past, present and future
unfold.
Looking deep into her soul, to see her
stories untold, wanting her, needing her
suppressing your innermost thoughts for
her.
Feeling your emotions always inclining,
always trying to be her friend, while inside slowly dying.
Seeing many of her relationships come to a
hurtful end, but you never make your move,
and in the end, she's still a
friend.
Now she lies in the hands of another
while your feelings are still inclining,
yet you continue to smother your feelings,
while she still continues crying
for the right guy to please her,
and you're still not making your
Move.
She cries and cries,
why are you still not making your move?
What do you really have to lose? When she waiting for you to make
your move.
[§]

Huh?

Feb '05

I was born in the ghetto where no one seems
to hear you crying. People dying as crack
prices continue rising.
Think about the good times, trying to conquer
the bad. Thinking about the last time, I saw
my moms and my dad.
Was on the street bugging, just living, trying
to make a dime. Trying to make it through the
troubles, and just get mine. Thinking of a future
and the life that I wanted. Was this change for me?
or did I mess my life up more?
I open up my eyes wider to see what I have, more
friends, a better life and mad love from my dad.
More bills then a nineteen year old really should have.
Bored out my mind, my are pockets inclining.
A man I am becoming, losing my childlike ways
Hardheaded still I am but slowly changing my ways.
Grew up too ignorant, and pride was strong in me.
Never trusting anyone, afraid my enemy they
would become too quickly.
I am deciding on my own that today's the day
that I start to change my life and change my
childish ways.

[§]

Do You Really Know a Person?

Feb '06

A pool of blood and pieces of flesh,
the killer did his best.
You kept him close and held him tight,
while knowing as we rested.

A day passes; you're coming home.
You find the house a mess.
Cops soon at your door and the floor a bloody mess.
Not listening to the banging, you follow the bloody path.
Tears filling your eyes, as you see your son and his dad.

As you, remember your family's past
every male to this day,
All killers of his past,
true murderers 'til this day.
A pain in your chest reveals you're not the last.
Your own son a murderer . . .
maybe because of your past.

But the future will reveal that you won't be the last.
Falling to the ground is where you breathe your last.
And you "knew" him.

[§]

Rambling about Life
July '03

People already see that life is a struggle,
beyond comparison, just like two worlds clashing.
A fight between an unimaginable heaven and hell.
Nowhere to go, because everyone knows that
everyone's dying.
People still outside crying, when their life's not shining,
because the Lord won't help them when they're outside lying.
False tears for too many years will get you
stuck in a ditch with brand new tears and brand
new fears.
Bloodstains on a shirt in the aftermath, will have
you trying to envision how another person's life
has passed.
Too many years have gone by as people have died,
and others' suicide attempts just to survive.
Many people feel like they'll never die; while
other people in life just want to die.
When it's the other people in life that makes them want to die,
not realizing this
as they're living their life.
[§]

Oh Daddy
April '05

I loved you for the man that you were - a straight thug.
Beat my ass 'til it was numb. Showing hard love.
I shed tears and screamed, "Stop!"
You just continued and cried, telling me you couldn't stop with my young badass.
I got a little older and smarter, but a young boy still. Trying to teach me a lesson but 'o a pain, still I am.
No whippings no more, just throws and slams,
telling me to calm down because too bad, I am.
I threw my fist up and thought that I was way too strong.
I threw a fist and missed and went down real strong.
The pain in my chest made me fall to the floor.
I tried to get up and fight. You said, "Son, no more".
Trying to be a man and shed not one tear,
how could I be wrong, as long as my pops is here?
Older and older, grown man, now.
Tears on my face, slowly calming down.
No more fighting. Educated by life, the son you once knew, no more wants to fight.
And the lessons you never taught me are stuck in my soul, and when my son is born. These lessons, he'll be told.

[§]

Gods Got You
June '06

Stop . . . Breath, what's really on your mind?
What the next person is thinking. Or are you
individually inclined?
This I really doubt because
subconsciously in your mind you want to look and
be the best standing in the church line.
Looking at another and downing their looks. Not knowing
that her stepfather beats her and never cooks. She's more
worried 'bout being fed, then looking all nice.
And all you can say is, "Look at her; she know she wrong! Looking
like a kid from a Save the Children commercial."
And today, two months later, your father left your mother.
Your mother's now on welfare. And with your father, your car.
Struggling to get by, you're no more the best.
The girl that had it all, is now like all the rest.
And the Save the Children girl?
Well, now she drives your car.
And as she drives around,
She thanks the Lord for your father. Did you learn a lesson?
[§]

Intensity
July 07

The intensity of your heartbeat slowly increasing,
breathe rate deepening, sweat beads forming ever so gently.
Body heat creeping to an incline of pure intimate passion,
legs trembling, body quaking, as your mind state starts spacing.
Lips licked, palms wet, and warmness in your legs,
the gentle touch of a feather makes your mind start to beg.
Lost thoughts of soft lips, gentle touches and soft licks.
The wetness of your lips; would be perfect for a quick slip.
Slow rubs from your chest to your back leave your body restless,
as the slow licks from your thighs to your stomach,
Slowly increases the sensation,
the thrusting of our bodies combines from our unknown temptation,
enters us into a continued quest of sexual confrontation.
Too far to stop, as we are too early to quit,
the urge that we feel sends us into an open abyss.
Our bodies start to moan as our lips meet gently.
decreasing the moment, we have had ….of sexual intensity. [§]

The Letter and the Dream
Nov 07

Many thoughts of you compound my mind,
your beauty, your thoughts, and our souls intertwined.
To hold you, to kiss you, to make your heart mine,
the very thought of you brings enlightenment into my life,

As tears start to fall, not on my face, but in my soul.
I ask the lord above why something so precious I cannot hold.
moments pass, as the sun goes dark, thunder rolls and there's
calmness in the dark.

"My son I say". "Answers for me, this question I ask
and answer truthfully."

When times are hard and she starts to cry, can you comfort her
and care for her and take pain from her life. . . .

"Lord!"
"My Son" Wait!

"When she is all alone on those dark cold nights her body is
cold and timing is not right." Can she call on you to please her, not
sexually but mentally and spiritually and make everything all right?"

This …is my question.

My chest goes heavy, my legs get weak, my mind goes blank and I
fall to my knees ….as silence fills the air.

As my eyes start to open, and I look down and the letter, she enters the
room. I quickly ball up the letter. I grab her and hug, as her as tears
fill my eyes. I kiss her lean back look stare at her deeply. " I love you my love
and I will always try."
YOU, are MY letter. [§]

Intimate Dreams
August 08

You are the illustration of god's beauty, the love in your eyes, the warmth of your lips, and the essence of which your soul fabricates.

The very essence of your soul grapples me in an unknown indulgence that interrupts the very meaning of my being.

So untouched and unseen your beauty is unmatched, from your succulent breast, to your lips, as I gasp, my mind starts to drift as I gazed in your eyes, craving you, wanting you, just to be inside.

An you quake, your mind starts pacing as my heart starts thumping, increasing as the water flows, your body starts to moan, as your legs spread wider, tempting to be overthrown.

So lost and intimate we caress each other, overwhelm by the ecstasy through touching and rubbing,

Gentle scratches to the back as I gaze into your eyes, leading us deeper into passions abyss as I rise. [§]

Dedication

This is dedicated to those individuals who have something to say, but are shut down because of their coyness or blocked by the judgment of others and to the Lord who allows us to speak without restraint. And Jocelynn Jason a promoter of free speech, knowledge, and wisdom. May children continue to learn under her standard. And people learn the true meaning of free speech.

To Be Continued,

The Question
Mar. 07

Locked heart and lost keys she laugh's with fake glee, to stop confrontation from those always asking. "What's wrong, Just smile"
She gives a little smirk not really worth her wild.
Actually annoyed by the presence of this person she turns and start conversations with another.
Is she really a name, for not opening herself , to a person that may only want one thing?
To mentally abuse for her sexual input. Or be the male that respects her and befriends her and stays put?
Are not all females promiscuous and inclined to seek and random encounter? Or are men just overbearing looking for a woman to tame.
The answer to these questions may one day be answers but not today because of our strong hold on the double standard.
We all are equal and want the same; but as times have changed only the aroused remain.
We often . . . .

Imagine
June 07

Wanting her, but not knowing her;
you know not what to expect.
Her eyes gaze upon yours
and more interested is what you get.
Her beauty is divine, and her accent shows all.
Education in her background, when talking you must stand tall.
Her beautiful lips so divine and succulent;
that they draw you near and have you begging for more.
Her curvaceous body makes most men dream of,
and erotic fantasy with rose peddles and more.
Too tender to fuck. You must caress, lick, and kiss.
Gentle body rubs to her back could bring her body total bliss.
Slow natural licks of the clit will her mind state racing,
body gyrating
soon your tongue will need replacement . . . .

Questions or comments:

Email :

- StephonStaley@ymail.com
- StephonStaley@gmail.com

The following pages are provided for your thoughts and experiences

www.ingramcontent.com/pod-product-compliance
Ingram Content Group UK Ltd.
Pitfield, Milton Keynes, MK11 3LW, UK
UKHW041837200726
13854UKWH00003BA/1183

9 780557 052776